By the Editors of Consumer Guide®

Grease Machines

Manufactured in the United States of America.
12345678910

Library of Congress Catalog Card Number: 78-71947

ISBN: 0-517-275708

This edition published by:
Beekman House
A Division of Crown Publishers, Inc.
One Park Avenue
New York, N.Y. 10016
By arrangement with Publications International, Ltd.

Two kinds of stars
appeared in the skies —
the rock 'n' rollers
and the metal benders

The Guitar And The Torch

The Great Depression was just the name of a sad story told by older people; the war was over. Teenagers and young adults of the 1950s and early '60s felt good about life. They felt like *moving*, and they needed a new beat. So they took parts of folk music, blues, gospel and country-western, poured them into a giant malted-milk-shake machine and whipped them up. It was loud and it was cool. It was rock 'n' roll.

The guys took to wearing black-leather jackets and ducktails; the girls, felt skirts and ponytails.

As much a symbol of the new life style as any of this was the car. Civilian automobile production had resumed at the end of the war, and the designers strained their imagination. Soon cars sprouted fins and great chunks of chrome. The automobile became a means of expressing individualism—especially for the young people.

Just as they'd created a new music with drums and electric guitars, young people reworked their cars with hammers and blowtorches. Their wheels, as well as their rhythms, were fast and free.

The stock automobiles of the '50s were called lead barges by the kids. They either bulged with oversized metal trim and fins or were shapeless. Most were big and bulky, sluggish, and difficult to maneuver. It's little wonder

George Barris, King of the Kustomizers, poses with one of his wildest creations, the Kopper Kart. Krazy, man.

that the young people took it upon themselves to change the cars they thought were boring. Even though many of the changes they made didn't improve a car's performance, customizers believed they were creating things of beauty. And if individuality was their goal, they succeeded.

The hero of the day was the nonconformist, whether he was a rock 'n' roll star, a movie star like James Dean, or the guy from the neighborhood who drove the wildest set of wheels. The guys with the coolest cars were the guys who made it with the slickest chicks.

Elvis Presley, and Dean in *Rebel Without A Cause,* were the envy of the young men, the heartthrobs of the women. But they were far away. The kid down the block, though, who could handle a torch, contour a fender, drop a frame and make a once-gutless engine outscreech everybody else's tires was as much a rebel, as much a celebrity. When not in his car, he could be recognized by the grease under his fingernails and the grease in his hair.

In the early days of the automobile, there were literally hundreds of manufacturers producing cars in a tremendous variety of designs and styles. Over the years there have been as many as 2500 manufacturers of automobiles in this country alone. The heyday of *choice* by the individual was in the early 1930s when certain cars had reached a design excellence that even today gives them unbelievable value as collectors' prizes. But the Great Depression swallowed up all but a few major companies.

The individual had had a wide selection of cars to suit his tastes. But as the depression killed off some of the companies and the war suspended car production, young car buyers relied on their own ingenuity to provide them with personalized automobiles. The custom-car craze was born.

The young men who were skilled with the torch and who had a driving determination to express themselves could translate their ideas into sheet metal with their own hands. Those with less ability satisfied their urge to create custom cars by turning the job over to one of the professional customizers of the period.

There was an army of backyard body benders doing business by the end of the '50s. In the late '40s and early

'50s, however, perhaps only a handful were destined to earn celebrity status.

Names like Bill Cushenbery, Joe Bailon, Darryl Starbird, Gene Winfield, Dick Korkes and Joe Wilhelm come to mind, but the best known of all was an enterprising fellow named George Barris. He converted a school hobby into a thriving business and earned himself the title "King of the Kustomizers."

Typical of the guy who was a youngster during the depression, Barris had been fascinated by cars ever since he wore knee britches. His first car was a dilapidated 1925 Buick. He'd straightened the mangled fenders, sewn the interior back together, and given the exterior a spectacular paint job of orange and blue with diagonal stripes in rainbow hues. This absolutely wild creation caused more comment and spectator interest than anything he had ever tackled before.

The artistry of the automotive painter on display: everything from tasteful stripes to the most outlandish kind of flames were part of the customizer's repertoire.

He advanced from the old Buick to a '29 Model A Ford roadster. This time, he hung extra lights on the front, installed winged ornaments, and attached foxtails. It was cool, man.

Easter vacation would find Barris in his crazy roadster, and a score of his buddies in similar cars, down at Balboa Island—a recreation center south of Los Angeles. There, in the parking lot outside the Rendezvous Ballroom, these guys and their chicks would hold impromptu car shows. This became a yearly ritual. Although local authorities around Newport Beach might have developed a few ulcers from the goings-on, the customized cars were a sensation among the younger set.

Barris learned the tricks of the metal-bending trade by hanging around a local body and fender shop. He got ahold of a '36 Ford coupe and applied his newly found knowledge of metal cutting, grinding, reshaping, torch welding, body paneling, and leading. The '36 Ford was a popular model even in its original form, but Barris changed the taillights, added skirts and ripple disks, simplified the grille, took off all of the exterior handles, and installed electric push-button doors and rear decklid. The modifications weren't much compared to what would come in later years, but back in 1940 it was real pioneering.

Then came World War II. Barris and others like him closed up shop for the duration. As soon as things settled down at war's end, Barris tackled a '36 Ford convertible. This involved removing the running boards (remember those?), molding different taillights, shaping a new housing for the rear license plate, adding custom "skirts" for the rear wheel openings, installing the emblems and door handles, and chopping the top. Chopping was new at the time, and it caused quite a stir.

By now, Barris Kustoms was fairly well established as a shop in a suburb of Los Angeles. Barris' fame began to spread following a hot rod and custom car show at the Los Angeles Armory. Pictures of the cars he had modified had appeared in the first issue of a magazine called *HOT ROD* in 1948. The magazine was sold at this show, and several of Barris cars were on display there. This was the beginning of the national recognition of two fast-growing hobbies; customizing and hot-rodding.

From that initial hot rod and custom car show in 1948,

Barris skyrocketed to fame. People in the entertainment world soon found him, and he built cars for such notables as Lionel Hampton, Liberace, Don Wilson and Rochester of the Jack Benny show, and George Raft. And through the '50s customs were built by Barris for Bobby Darin, Jayne Mansfield, Elvis Presley, Dwayne Hickman and Tony Curtis, to name a few.

Some of his customs became well-known across the nation. They were displayed at hot rod and custom car shows as the craze spread eastward. His Golden Sahara was one of these, and it established some styling firsts. Built in 1954, the car had bumper bullets, then new, which later came out on production Cadillacs and became famous. It had a checkered grille, later seen on the '55 Ford. The thin-line rear fender fins, also new then, later became popular on more than one make produced in Detroit. The spare tire well, molded into the rear decklid, appeared on Chrysler Imperials 1957-58 models.

One of his customs was a pacesetter for pickups. Built by Barris in 1956, the Kopper Kart pickup probably was one of the biggest attractions of all time at shows around the country. Originally it was a '55 Chevy pickup. But by the time Barris had finished with it, it bore no resemblance to the truck produced in Detroit. Its body was sectioned; its top was chopped; and its panels were contoured, sculptured, and reshaped. Much of Barris' styling innovations were picked up by Detroit and even today their influence is evident on production cars.

Another professional customizer of the '50s was an enterprising car designer named Darryl Starbird. He purchased his first car, a 1941 Ford convertible, while in high school, and immediately began restyling the car in

1

his dad's home workshop in Wichita, Kansas.

On his first attempt, Starbird installed a Chrysler kit with a large '48 Chrysler rear bumper and fender skirts, and altered the springs and shocks to give the car a radical "rake"—the "in" modification of the time. This custom wasn't exactly a show-stopper, but it was a beginning, and Starbird creations of later years went on to establish him as a talented designer.

For instance, he was the first to come up with the "bubble," a contoured plastic top that was about as futuristic as you could get in those days. He customized a Corvair in this manner and gave it a name, the Forcasta. For another one-of-a-kind custom, Starbird created a double bubble, with flip-down doors, a single headlight, and three wheels. It looked like the '50s image of a flying saucer.

Starbird received national recognition for his work on a '47 Cadillac and a '55 Plymouth. In 1959, he won the Top Body Achievement Award at the National Hot Rod Association's National Custom Car Show at Detroit for his restyling of a 1956 Ford Thunderbird. His show cars all had fancy names, like Predicta and Fantabula.

In the late '50s and early '60s, Starbird's Star Kustom Shop in Wichita became a center of influence for futuristic customs in the southern midwest. His later cars were handbuilt from the chassis up. They earned for him a reputation that was seldom matched by anyone else in the business.

Another pro in the custom car building business was Gene Winfield of Modesto, California. Windy's Custom Shop was going strong in 1948. One of his first customs was a Model T roadster. It was shown in the very first

Oakland (California) Roadster Show in 1949.

Uncle Sam grabbed Winfield in 1950 for a tour of duty during the Korean conflict, but that didn't put an end to Winfield's interest in customizing. He and a buddy chopped and sectioned a 1941 Ford coupe and did other custom work while they were stationed in Japan. Winfield reopened his shop when he got back to the States.

From about 1955 on, Winfield's customs often were top winners at custom shows. His restyled 1962 Pontiac Bonneville won the "Car d'Elegance" award at the Oakland Show in 1962. Modifications included quad headlights, extended front and rear fenders, handmade taillights, a molded-in front grille, and a "clean-swept" body. Another one of his top customs was a modernistic Mercury which featured a sectioned body, '59 Chrysler rear fenders grafted onto the rear, plastic fins, and wedge-shaped taillights.

Winfield's Solar Scene custom was a radical modification of a '49 Mercury. It had sculptured wheel wells; molded-in quad, vertical headlights; tubular "floating" grille; inlaid bumpers; and a front seat that swung out when the door was opened.

In the mid-1950s, two brothers opened an establishment called Custom City in the heart of Motor City—Detroit. Larry and Mike Alexander went into the business of taking a standard production car and, by revamping the styling and design, producing cars that were unique.

One of their restyled cars, a 1956 Ford, was chosen one of the 10 best customs to be built during 1956 by a popular automotive hobby magazine. The changes involved a grille made from Studebaker shells; a wrap-around, one-piece front bumper that was centered in the

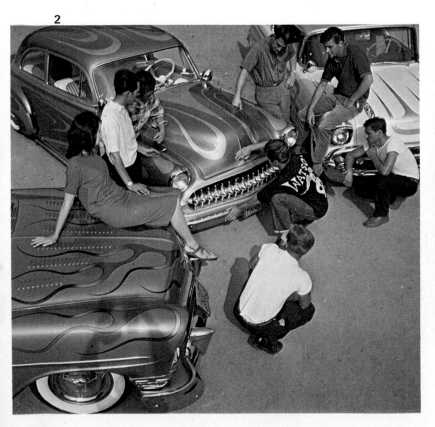

Part of the 1950s customizing era were the Ford Deuce (1), shown here with moon discs and a Chrysler hemi; '53 Chevys given the scalloping treatment, such as these (2) painted by Larry Watson; and flames, like these (3) painted on a chopped '50 Mercury. As much a part of the '50s were ducktail haircuts, T-shirts and shades. Cars were just one way that young people of the decade expressed their individualism.

grille opening; Olds headlights; and enclosing housing for the side exhaust pipes. It wasn't considered a radical custom, but it had wide appeal because of its clean lines and quality of workmanship.

Bill Cushenbery is another customizer who achieved fame in the '50s. Originally, he worked with Darryl Starbird in Wichita. Then Cushenbery went west to Monterey, California, and created his own brand of customs.

He won singular recognition for the work he did on a 1940 Ford coupe. El Matador, as it was called, had a very low silhouette—accomplished by a 3½-inch chopping of the top and a 4½-inch body section. The car's most interesting styling features were contoured fenders that contained quad, canted headlights up front; and a rolled-pan, contoured body section at the rear.

Probably the most visible evidence of customizing all through the '50s was created by painters. Von Dutch was one of the first, best known for his wild pin-striping of customs in the late '40s and early '50s. Some tried to imitate him; others created fanciful painting concepts of their own. Big Daddy Ross had a talent for wild colors, cartooning, striping. Dean Jefferies was another painter, as was Larry Watson. Jefferies and Watson went in for flame painting, scallops, striping and other intricate designs and detailing.

Pin-striping got started in the mid-1950s and swept the country by storm. Flame painting and scalloping followed.

Flames began with little flickers that emanated from the hood louvers of some of the earlier customs, but they soon spread to envelop the entire car. The flames often were made to look like the real thing. Many colors, ranging from a blazing red through orange to a brilliant yellow, were blended and hand rubbed, tipped with gold, and finished off with contrasting stripes.

Flames evolved into scalloping. This more subdued form of painting was designed with care and comparatively good taste. The imagination of the man with the brush was extraordinary, and this alone controlled the results as they ran the gamut from paint blotches to pure ingenuity.

For a true lover of cars, the decade of the '50s was a great time to live. Big changes took place in production cars in just 10 years, and credit for plenty of those changes can be given to the custom car builders. They may have been metalworkers by trade, but restyling was their hobby and goal, and if they obtained some degree of recognition from their peers for their efforts, they felt amply rewarded.

But this book is not intended just for people who consider themselves car lovers. These customized machines are much more than merely souped-up cars; they're symbols of a new-found freedom. They represent the creativity, the nonconformity, the rebellious nature of young people who were determined to have a good time.

To understand the kids of the '50s, you have to do more than listen to records by Elvis Presley and Buddy Holly, watch movies like *The Wild One* and *Rebel Without A Cause,* and recall sock hops and Sweet Sixteen parties. You've got to think about the cars of the day.

Imagine the guys slipping into their leather jackets and running a comb through their ducktails one last time. Imagine them cruising over to their chicks' house and bopping to the best of "Hound Dog" and "Peggy Sue" on the car radio. And as you flip through the following pages, imagine yourself strolling around a custom car show with hundreds of these guys and gals.

The year is 1957 or thereabouts. You've returned to the days of the Grease Machines. Dig it.

The 1950 Ford is wearing a new set of fins installed by a customizer. The gal is wearing Capri pants; the guy, a flat-top and white bucks.

Glossary of Customizing Terms

Chopped, channeled, nosed, frenched—these are terms that haven't been in use much in the past few years. But they were used extensively by automotive customizers in the 1950's to describe the wild effects they created. We use the terms throughout the book, so we felt a glossary was in order. Here are brief definitions of the customizer's terms.

Channeling: The dropping of a car's body inside of the framework, to give the effect that the car is floating just a fraction of an inch over the ground.

Chopping: The cutting down of a car's roofline by means of a removal of sheet metal; sometimes so drastic that the windshield was little more than a slit.

Decking: Removal of all the trim—license plate bracket, trunk handle, etc.—from the rear of the car and filling of the holes.

Frenching: The recessing of lights—taillights or headlights—by a change in the sheet metal or the building up of a flange around the lights.

Lowering: An alteration of a car's suspension to bring the body very near the ground, making the car look as though it is almost dragging on the pavement.

Nosing: The removal of all the chrome from a hood and the filling of holes.

Sectioning: The cutting of all body panels around the car to decrease their height; sometimes used in combination with lowering.

TV-TIME TUDOR

Park It And Watch "Your Hit Parade"

When this custom was built, the owner announced that it was the first of many 1950 Ford coupes he would restyle in a similar fashion. Whether or not he followed through is not known, but his prototype certainly incorporates some refreshing design concepts.

The front styling is set off by quad headlights, employing '57 Chrysler units fitted into reshaped front fenders. The rear taillights were from a '57 Olds 98. The hood was shaved, and concave side scoops were made to blend in with the contour of the headlights. The floating-type grille consists of bars set in a cavity of sheet metal and tubing.

Sheet metal has been sculptured on the rear decklid to conceal the license plate light and deck latch. The door handles have been removed: the doors latch by push buttons that are electrically controlled.

For the picnic outing, a TV set in the trunk works off a voltage converter. Reversed '54 Dodge side trim matches the stylish Mercury rear wheel well skirts. Exhaust pipes extend along the side rocker panels.

White and wine-red vinyl graces the interior as well as the luggage compartment. The dash is padded and also covered in white. The interior garnish moldings have been chromed.

Caddy Catalina

Customized '52 Pontiacs Were So Rare

A neat transformation has been accomplished on this rarely restyled 1952 Pontiac Catalina hardtop. The custom features a cut-down Chevy grille installed with an Olds top bar, Cadillac headlights modernized with hoods, and a power plant that gives it plenty of go.

The wheel wells are altered to give the car the illusion of being lower, and the wheels themselves are dressed up with wire spokes and a bullet center.

At the rear, '56 Olds taillights from a 98 model fit into extended rear fenders. Bumper guards have been removed to give the machine a cleaner look. Spotlights and a hood that's been peaked and louvered complete the fine exterior.

The interior is plush with padding, pleats, and diamond-tufted vinyl.

This machine is one real goer. The young fellow, sporting his own flat-top with fenders, shows us that the stock Pontiac engine is gone. Living under the hood now is a full-race Cadillac V8, which transfers its power to the rear wheels through a '37 LaSalle floor-shift transmission.

Flamboyant Fairlane

NJA 936

Seven Scoops,
Seven Different
Flavors

Body sculpturing continued to progress as the decade of the '50s drew to a close. A startling example of this type of styling is this 1957 Ford two-door.

The least radical alteration to the custom was the simple but handsome tubular bar grille. Headlights and taillights were deeply tunneled and trimmed with unusual bird-like beaks. Seven scoops up front and in back were also a part of the styling.

The base color of the car was gold-green over which scalloping was applied in gold, lime gold, lavender, burgundy, candy apple, Chinese blue and red. All of the scalloping was then outlined with a thin white line.

To make the car go, the engine was modified with an Iskenderian cam, Offenhauser three-carburetor manifold, and Magspark ignition. The power plant was also bored and fully balanced.

One of the early customs created in the Southland is this 1950 Chevrolet two-door, modified by Larry Watson (who became well known as a car-painting artist). This car has been painted two-tone purple.

Changes include the installation of multiple '53 Chevy grille teeth in a molded-in grille shell, headlight styling lifted from a '55 Oldsmobile, and a hood that's nosed and slightly peaked. The bumper guards have been removed and the V-type windshield has been replaced with a one-piece Olds glass.

The popped-out flipper on the hubcaps is wild. Inverted Mercury taillights were borrowed from a '54 model, and they are mounted low in extended rear fenders. Both

Lavender Low~Rider

Southland Gives Birth To The Purples

rear deck and doors are push-button operated.

Heart-shaped and pleated vinyl upholstery dresses up the interior, as does a white steering wheel and plastic control knobs on the dash.

The spear-shaped side trim shown here was a favorite with customizers of the '50s, as were chromed side exhausts. Here, the pipes extend from the front wheel well to a point just forward of the rear wheel well. (Skirts were sometimes added to the rear wheel wells to give the illusion that the car was dragging, as sometimes they actually were.)

The fancy scallops were an added touch, applied after the neat custom had seen the road for awhile in the mid-1950s.

Rebel Without A Flaw

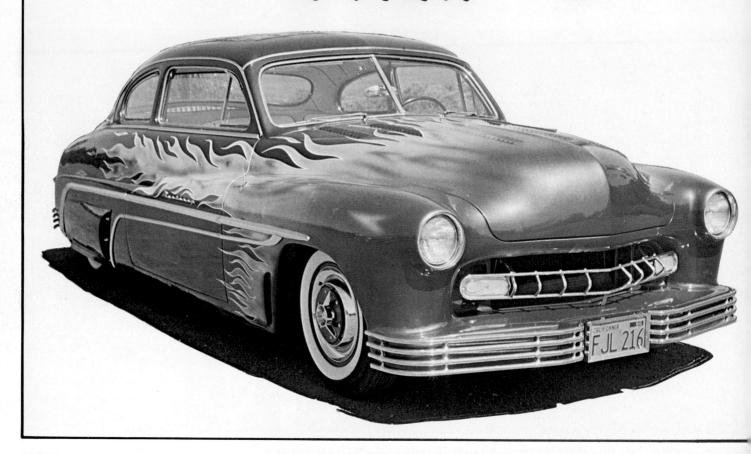

The Some-Like-It-Hot Monterey

Roaring rearward like the blast from a rocket, the spectacular flame painting on this 1950 Mercury Monterey is only one part of its distinctive styling. The owner spent three years and over $2000 on modifications of this set of wheels, which resembles the car driven by James Dean in *Rebel Without A Cause.*

The hood is peaked and perforated with no fewer than 120 louvers. Front and rear bumpers are styled from tubular stock, hand-formed to wrap the reshaped gravel pans.

Of special interest is the way the '56 Chrysler taillights were molded into the rear fenders at a 45-degree angle.

To emphasize the low lines, side trim from a '55 DeSoto Firedome is shaped to sweep back and drop sharply fore and aft of the rear fender skirts. Exhaust tips exit at the ends of the DeSoto chrome. Scoops are built into the forward edges of the skirts and trimmed with short chromed spears on the body panels.

Wheel discs are made up from Dodge Lancer and Edsel components.

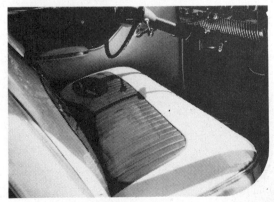

Magnificent
Modified
Mayflower

**Plymouth Rocks
To A
Different Beat**

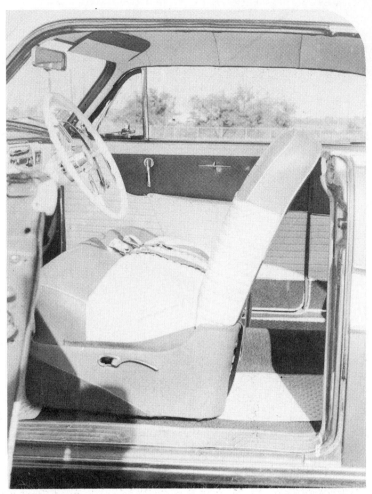

A custom doesn't have to look like a machine from outer space to be accepted as one of the best. Neatness and simplicity in design of the restyling are characteristics of some of the best customs of the '50s.

This 1951 Plymouth Belvedere hardtop qualifies as tasteful. The car masquerades with assorted components. A Mercury-type grille has replaced the original, and the headlights are from a '57 Olds. The side trim was borrowed from a '55 Olds 98; the rear bumper comes from a '55 Plymouth.

Major modifications restyled the rear end of the car with pleasing effects. The rear fenders were extended to accept '55 Plymouth taillights, and the spare tire was mounted continental fashion.

Blue and white vinyl upholstery dresses up the interior. The wheel discs carry the monogram of the car's owner. Dual spotlights and chrome nose molding provide the finishing touches for this Plymouth rocker.

Vivacious VICKIE

Ground-Hugging Hardtop In Passion Purple

Custom cars were made to hug the ground in the mid-1950s. This 1952 Ford Victoria does so, about as tightly as possible. The radical lowering job has been accomplished by reworking the front spindle support arms and C-ing the frame. The driveshaft tunnel at the rear has been dropped. The floating-type grille shell is made of sheet metal and '53 Chevy grille parts. A single bar, parking lights and grille teeth have been "floated" into it.

Other small chrome teeth have been located in the air scoops at the leading edges of the front fenders. The headlight rims are borrowed from a '55 Chevy. The front fenders extend over them, forming a lip. A chromed exhaust pipe runs the full length of the body to the forward edge of each of the rear fender scoops. The taillights come from a '55 Lincoln.

Spinner-type hubs adorn the wheels; teardrop spotlights add an extra touch of chrome.

Other modifications include a molded rear gravel pan, upholstered rear package shelf, and a trunk completely upholstered in pleated purple and white vinyl. More vinyl and deep-pile carpeting give a look of class to the passenger compartment.

Flaming Fireball

Buick Special Goes To Blazes

Can you imagine using 20 rolls of masking tape to paint a car? Well, that's what it took to do the flames on this 1957 Buick Special hardtop.

The yellow, orange and red flames are a true work of art, completely overshadowing all the other modifications performed on this custom. Yet without the other changes, the owner probably felt his car was not worthy of being among 'em.

The hood has been nosed and peaked; the trunk has been decked. Chrome wire wheels are used, and all window moldings have been chromed. The beautiful Buick is equipped with Appleton spots and lake pipes that flank the undersides from front wheel well to rear. The grille is copper-plated, as are the taillights.

The Leprechaun

Imp Wears A
Coat Of
Green And Gold

In the later 1950s, customs began to be restyled with less metalwork than had been "in" earlier. A pleasing example of this type of moderate change is the 1958 Chevrolet Impala hardtop shown here.

The car's owner has expressed himself by installing taillights from a '52 Pontiac in fenders that have been slightly extended and peaked. Most of the chrome trim has been removed, along with the door handles. The car has also been nosed and decked to give it a super-clean look.

The glimmer of chrome has been added at the wheels, by means of Dodge Lancer hubcaps; and at the sides with chrome stacks.

The interior and luggage compartment have been completely reupholstered in tuck and roll with gold and white vinyl.

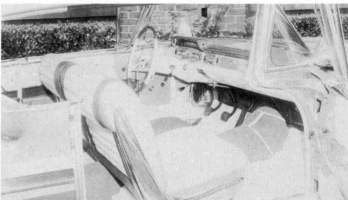

By the late 1950s, customizers had already modified scores of 1955 Thunderbirds, the two-seaters that were Ford's contribution to the sports car market.

This 1955 T-Bird's modifications cost about $7500—and that was a heap of money in 1959, the year this custom hit the streets. The front end features a grille made of conduit bar stock, twin conduit bumpers, quad headlights in a hand-formed shell, dual front fender scoops that contain chrome "teeth," and a hood airscoop that has been given similar treatment.

The rear end also has been modified extensively. The alterations include extended rear fenders over '53 Lincoln taillights, and a conduit-formed bumper that is similar in style to the one up front. The wheels have been reversed, and are covered with special bullet-type hubcaps.

The interior features matching red and white vinyl, and red rugs. Side exhaust stacks, a popular customizing innovation of the '50s, add some flash to the T-Bird's profile.

BIG BUCK$ T-BIRD

For This Bird, The Sky's The Limit

SCALLOPED BIG M

CALIFORNIA 56
FNX 139

Merc's Paint Job
Started A Fad

By the late 1950s, customizing had taken on a new dimension as a result of intricate paint designs which accentuated most anything that needed accentuating. Denoting speed, of course, was a major reason for graceful curves, tapering spears, and all the rest of the innovations that flowed from the painter's brush.

This 1956 Mercury hardtop was a forerunner of the fad that swept the nation.

Yet it is gracefully executed and has stood up well with the passage of time. The scallops, done in a vivid red on the Arctic white exterior, have an appealing design. They don't take away from the body work that makes the car unique.

The extended rear fenders incorporate huge vertical Packard taillights, fused together in pairs. The rear bumper has been simplified by the removal of the usual guards.

P01167

Who said hobbies don't pay off? At the height of the customizing era, a young fellow named Larry Watson converted his artistic talents from the canvas to sheet metal. He soon moved up from a jalopy Ford to the 1959 Cadillac hardtop shown here.

It all started after school, down at the back-alley garage. The fad then was pinstriping. Every kid in the neighborhood wanted the new thin-line striping on his car, and the craze criss-crossed the country in less than a year. Striping at first was conservative.

It wasn't long before intricate designs, shapes, and colors became commonplace. In a year or so, flames spread over the customs. After that came scallops. Watson and other painters like him were making money like crazy.

This neatly scalloped Cadillac is a car that has been only moderately modified otherwise. It's been lowered, nosed and decked. And spotlights have been added.

Simple but beautiful—that's Larry Watson's Caddy.

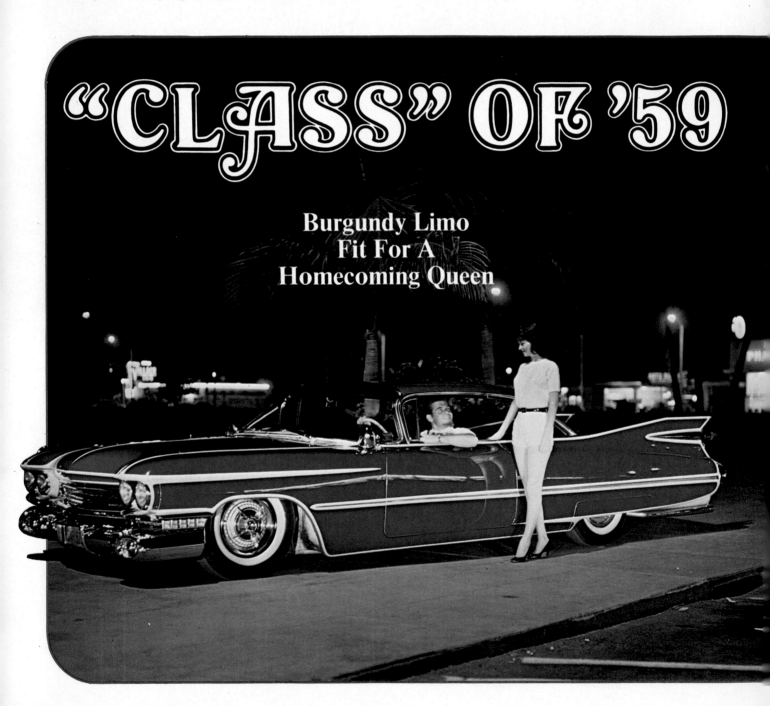

"CLASS" OF '59

Burgundy Limo Fit For A Homecoming Queen

CANDY APPLE COUPE

'53 Ford Looks
Good Enough To Eat

The customizer of this '53 Ford Club Coupe has taste—a taste for candy. The exterior paint job is the car's best feature. It's a study in conservatism: two-tone candy apple red with tangerine, outlined with thin-line white striping. The interior of the coupe has been redone to match the outside—white vinyl upholstery piped in black for the seats, and red carpeting with white trim.

The Coupe carries a '54 Chevy grille with extra "teeth" welded on. Both front and rear bumpers were smoothed and the attaching bolts molded in to provide the desired one-piece look. Side trim consists of '50 Oldsmobile and '54 Mercury chrome spears.

The rear wheel wells are cut out and flared to match the front wheel wells. Hubcaps feature spinners around a center hub bullet.

In the early days of customizing, a few metal benders of the time became pretty well known for their restyling efforts. By the time this 1956 Chevy pickup was transformed into the Kopper Kart, the name George Barris was a household word among the car enthusiasts. The Kopper Kart creation brought Barris further fame.

Beautifying the Chevy truck was a major modification project, but to George Barris, who was an expert metalworker as well as a restyling innovator, it was all in the day's work.

Body modifications involve a 5½-inch section removal from the body and a 4-inch vertical removal from the top. The entire front design was formed by hand from sheet metal stock, mesh, and bars. The elaborate setup includes quad headlights installed in hooded shells, surrounded by a mesh grille; an electric eye in the center of the grille to control headlight high beams; a somewhat similar design at the rear which incorporates taillights and turn signals; sculptured hood, fenders, and body panels; elaborate tonneau covers; fancy interior with all sorts of electronic goodies; and other items that can make any custom car enthusiast drool.

KOPPER KART

Barris Goes Berserk With Chevy Truck

Visions Of Corvette

Same Body, Many Different Personalities

The Corvette, which was originally introduced in 1953, was not an immediate success. The first models were slow and stubby, but designers and engineers quickly recognized the car's shortcomings and began improving its looks and power.

It wasn't long before many customizers set to work on a 'Vette, toying with its styling and giving it even more get-up-and-go. Here are a few examples of what some skilled customizers can do with Corvettes.

Headlight assemblies have been reworked. Some 'Vettes have been given quad lamps; some have lamps that are recessed and

partially hidden behind wire mesh.

A variety of grille designs has been devised. They vary from those with a locomotive motif to those with some teeth in them to ultrasimple, floating configurations.

Different types of wheels and wheel covers—from chromed wheels to moon discs—are used to give each Corvette a look all its own. And, of course, each customizer has his own style of painting. The techniques range from simple two-toning to bold scallops to flames to sedate pinstriping.

The number of Corvette fans multiplied quickly toward the end of the decade.

DOLL BUGGY

Hit The Road In A
Fur-Filled Fairlane

This 1955 Ford custom is understated and classy on the outside, a bit wilder inside.

Its paint consists of a base of Burma green, and darker green used for the tasteful scallops. Pinstriping completes the paint job.

The front end has been modified only slightly by the installation of a mesh grille and horizontal chromed bars. Spotlights, side exhausts and chromed spinner hubs add extra glitter to the exterior.

Inside, the dash and rear-view mirror have been covered with a soft, white fur.

The tailfin was a styling innovation of the '50s that captured the imagination of customizers throughout the United States. Modifications made to many cars reflected this love for the big fin.

An excellent example of the trend is shown in this 1950 Buick. Its huge fins have been contoured and integrated with the rear fenders.

The fins are the most flamboyant changes, but many other modifications are part of this custom job. The front and rear bumpers have been assembled from separate chromed sections and inset into newly contoured front and rear body sections. Bullet taillights from a '55 Ford complement the bullets incorporated with each bumper section. Fine horizontal strips give class to the oval grille section.

The windshield and cowl have been taken from a '55 Buick, as has the dashboard. The headlight rims come from a '56 Lincoln.

Wonder With Wings

'50 Buick Gets The Big-Fin Treatment

Flaming Green Stovebolt

Chevy Shines
With Pipes And Paint

The transformation of this car just the way its owner wanted took 18 months and $800 of hard-earned money. Those long hours of tossing hamburgers at the local drive-in were well rewarded when the custom was complete.

Body changes are not revolutionary: the Chevy has simply been smoothed out. Neat louvers have been cut in the hood; emblems removed. It's been nosed and decked. Also, it's been lowered a full eight inches up front; six inches at the rear. Olds flipper wheel covers and 5.50 racing slicks dress up the car's running feet, and the engine has been balanced and given a 1/8-inch bore job. Dual four-barrels on the 283-cubic-inch power plant also add some guts.

The entire package is wrapped up in beautiful flames of green and red.

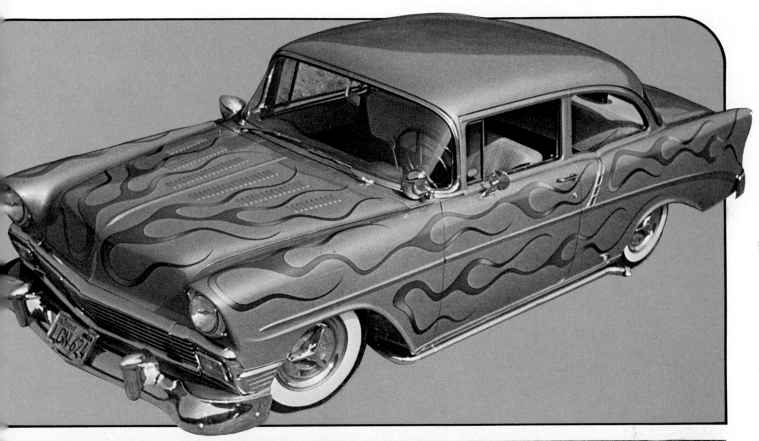

57-Karat Custom

Ford Glistens
With Trim
Of Gold

Chevy grille components were very popular with customizers of the late '50s. This 1957 Ford Fairlane 500 hardtop has been given an effective styling change at the front by the installation of vertical chrome teeth borrowed from Chevy.

The rear end has been given a unique appearance by bullet-shaped lenses in round taillight housings. And, of course, a scallop paint job provides the necessary highlights. Twin spotlights have also been installed.

Giving the Fairlane some unexpected touches of luxury are wheel covers and other trim items of gold.

These moderate modifications result in a car that is conservative and clean—an extremely attractive package for customizers who like their cars both wild and mild.

Lincoln In Disguise

**All Dressed Up
In A
Cadillac's Tux**

When the American luxury crown went to Cadillac, customizers who got their hands on one of the other luxurious makes would go to extremes to restyle their cars *à la* Caddy.

That's what has happened to this 1947 Lincoln. The radical modifications wipe out the car's original identity.

To give the car a Cadillac look in front, a windshield from a Caddy has been used; in the rear, the car sports Cadillac finned fenders. The spare tire is carried in a cutout on the rear deck, like a Continental. Inside, the convertible top has been fully lined for an added touch of class.

AIRSCOOPED IMP

Chrysler's Cool
And Continental

Stylized in a conservative manner, this 1952 Chrysler four-door sedan nevertheless qualifies as a true "grease machine."

The most radical change involves the cutting of a pair of airscoops in the peaked, louvered, and molded hood. Frenched-in headlights and a slightly modified grille (the "teeth" were removed) have been enhanced by the installation of a massive front bumper. A matching rear chrome bumper with Continental spare tire have been installed. The rear fenders are elongated, and vertically mounted bullet-type taillights have been installed. Side trim and all window moldings are chromed. Chromed wire wheels and wide white sidewalls dress up the side appearance.

Magnificent Mercury

The Smoothest Of Work On A Four-Door Merc

When the customizing fad hit America in the late '40s and early '50s, stock cars were bulbous and balloonlike. They had little real style. The young couldn't and didn't go along with it. Automobile enthusiasts took whatever body style they could get ahold of, and went to work smoothing, cutting, chopping and lowering, discarding parts and adapting replacements.

Ford products were a particular target—even the big Mercurys. This 1950 four-door Merc was not much to look at in its original configuration, but its owner came up with many updating ideas that work.

The front end has been restyled with louvers in the hood, hooded headlights with rims taken from a '57 Chevy, and a toothy grille taken from a '54 Chevy. Hardware on the hood, deck, and doors has been discarded and all seams filled. The windshield center post has been removed. The stock taillights are frenched into the rear fenders. Wheels are reversed, chromed, and fitted with custom discs that contain a clear plastic center bullet.

The interior sports a reupholstery job in silver vinyl and green carpeting. The dash is completely redone, padded, and covered with vinyl pleats. The only visible instrument is the speedometer.

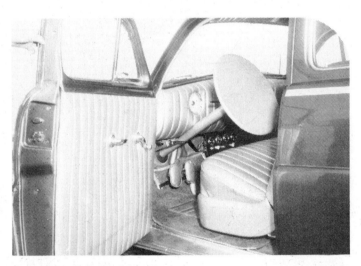

THE BEAK

'49 Chevy Resembles
A Bird Of Prey

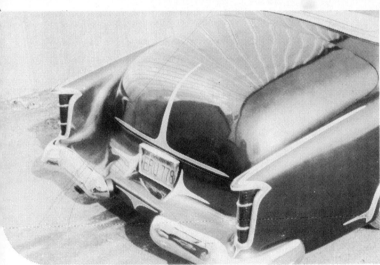

Distinctive shapes were a goal of many customizers in the early '50s. Some copied birds of prey. Such is the case with this 1949 Chevrolet custom, because of its bill-like extended headlight hoods.

The idea has been carried out also on the taillights. The rear fenders have been extended 14 inches, and Chrysler taillights are installed and frenched in. A two-piece Pontiac rear bumper with hand-formed gravel pan has been added to the rear. The rear treatment also involves a boxed-in license plate frame.

Other body modifications include the remolding of the fender wells and the addition of a special ornate airscoop grille on the forward section of each rear fender.

The overall appearance of the custom only remotely resembles a 1949 Chevrolet. That, of course, was the goal of many car owners who wanted something out of the ordinary. The continual search for individualism in their transportation, however, usually resulted in an actual improvement in overall looks, as this job certainly did.

The "borrowing" of parts from other makes usually helped create the distinctive touches. For instance, a '56 Chrysler grille has been inserted in the remolded front-end cavity; and the taillights are also '56 Chrysler.

On the inside, all-white rolled upholstery and a shag rug are used.

Chopped And Sectioned, Ford Looks Delicious

Banana Split

Here's a machine so radically sectioned and channeled that the customizer couldn't put a hood over the engine. The custom job began as a '40 Ford two-door. The original power plant has been replaced with a '57 Pontiac V8—chromed to be as much a source of beauty as power.

Chrome push bars up front replace the original bumpers, the side vents on the grille have been specially chromed, and the center of the grille is made up of gleaming chrome mesh.

At the back, the recessed license plate frame and "ducktail" rear end resemble the design that has appeared on Corvettes since this machine was built.

The reworked sheet metal has been given many coats of pearlescent yellow paint, and the interior has been dressed up with brown and white vinyl, rolled and pleated.

Peach Of A Dodge

Lancer's Paint Job Is Tasty

By the time this custom job was started, automobile styling was already on the wild side, so relatively few changes were needed to make this machine an eye-catcher.

All original exterior ornamentation has been removed, and the car's been nosed and decked. The center emblem in the hood, the trim around the headlights, and the wheel covers have been painted.

Teardrop spots and lake pipes have been installed, and the car has been lowered about three inches. (Chrysler torsion-bar cars such as this were lowered by means of a twist in the bars.)

The exterior has been given an attractive scalloping treatment.

Fifty~One A Nifty One

Highly Refined Sculpturing Makes It A Standout

Body sculpturing is highly refined in this 1951 Ford two-door, which was restyled in the mid-1950s.

Extensive revision of the front end involves the installation of Imperial quad headlights in a canted position, and '56 Chrysler horizontal grille bars in a newly shaped oval that is tied in with the headlight shells.

At the rear, the license plate housing is molded into an electrically operated rear decklid. The airscoop at the rear of the top ties in nicely with the trucklid styling. The taillights, with their partially enclosed hand-formed shells, provide distinctive styling to the peaked rear fenders.

Those reverse-curved sections aft of each wheel well and the neatly contoured "lip" that circumvents the area provide interesting distinction to an otherwise slab-sided body. Within these flared sections, a stainless steel filler is used.

The front bumpers, shortened '55 Pontiac units, have been molded into a reshaped area below the headlights and grille. Dodge Lancer side trim blends in nicely with the lipped wheel wells and flared sections.

The custom is painted a gold-green lacquer with accentuating scallops around the taillights and the hooded license plate section on the rear deck.

Bodacious Belair
Take A Look At Those Way-Out Fenders

Customizers in the early '50s often set styling trends. A prime example of neat customizing is this 1950 Chevy Belair.

Even though the modifications are very dramatic, the results in styling are conservative and in good taste. The lines are smooth; the overall appearance is appealing.

Drastic alterations to the front end reveal grafting of '53 Buick fenders onto the Chevy frame, installation of '53 Buick headlights, sculpturing and reshaping of the grille opening, and the inserting of 1953 DeSoto grille "teeth."

The rear treatment features extended rear fenders, reshaped to accept twin Corvette taillights on either side of the fender. The car has been lowered in front by cutting springs; in back by lowering blocks. Chrome conduit has been used for bumpers, shaped to encircle the fenders. Other pieces wrap around the bottom of the rear deck. Rear fender airscoops, side exhaust pipes, a recessed rear license plate pocket, reverse wheel rims, and electrical push-button hood and rear deck are also part of the modifications.

Hairy Hemi
Ford Gets A Flat-Top

The ingenuity of the customizers of the early '50s never seemed to end. Ford pheaton bodies were hard to come by, but that didn't stop one custom car enthusiast who wanted an open job with class. He merely took a Ford Victoria and chopped the entire top off to form the neat phaeton-bodied custom you see here.

The body has been carefully reworked and finished off with a fiberglass cowl, which accommodates a low V windshield. The chassis has been dropped three inches front and rear. The body finish is '57 Chrysler Cloud White lacquer. Dress-up items include Dodge Lancer discs, front and rear nerf bars, and upholstered running boards. Sandalwood and white vinyl upholstery is used in the interior.

The power plant, of course, isn't stock. It is a souped-up Chrysler hemi.

MIDNIGHT VAGABOND

**Blue, Blue Olds
Moves Out
After Dark**

The real glamour machines of the '50s were those cars that denoted stylized elegance in the modifications done by the customizers of the period.

A fine example of this is this 1955 Olds hardtop. Its midnight blue lacquer paint job shines through even in black-and-white.

The car has been shorn of all its original trim, emblems, ornaments and handles. Side trim from a '58 Ford has been added to create an elegant highlight. The front fenders are extended, and dual headlights have been installed in each housing tunnel. The grille was fashioned from molded-over copper tubing. Two airscoops have been cut into the forward section of the hood.

At the rear, the fenders also are extended and peaked to accommodate '59 Chrysler taillights. The rear bumper is set into a rolled pan, providing another unique styling feature.

Chrome exhaust pipes extend from flared pods molded into the front fenders and rocker panels.

'56 Dodge Truck Moves To The Big City

Peggy Sue's Pickup

The compelling urge and basic philosophy behind customizing in the decade of the '50s was to produce something different. The owner of this 1956 Dodge Pickup decided his drab machine was a fertile field for his ideas.

The basic identity of the pickup has been retained; then styling improvements were made. These consist of nosing the hood, adding twin side exhaust pipes, chroming the running boards, and creating a luxurious interior with coral and white vinyl. White covers are provided for the side-mounted spare and the pickup bed.

Partially for appearance sake and partially to lower the pickup for easy entry, the truck has been lowered front and rear by four inches. It's been painted coral and white with scalloped spears.

PNG 876

oHHHHHH poncho!

Scalloping Galloping Bonneville From Old California

In this case, the paint is the whole story. The 1958 Pontiac Bonneville hardtop has been given six completely different sets of scallops in lime gold, orange gold, candy apple red and silver; plus flames.

The other modifications to the car can be thought of as stock customizing for the era.

They include the installation of spotlights which, incidentally, also have been painted, and the more or less traditional side exhaust pipes on either side. The other restyled items are the taillights—they're '56 Olds units.

Any way you look at it, you notice this machine.

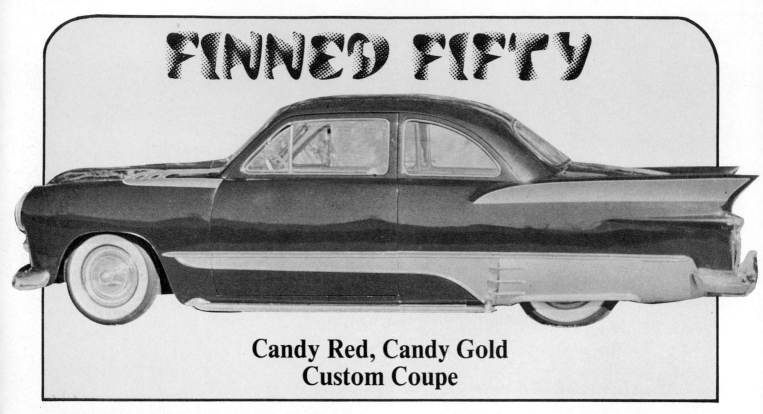

FINNED FIFTY

**Candy Red, Candy Gold
Custom Coupe**

In the early customizing years, body builders were always vying for recognition at car shows, and car enthusiast publications often contained sections displaying "The 10 Best Customs" of the year. One of the winners of such honors was this 1950 Ford two-door, restyled by Joe Bailon, one of the top customizers of the early '50s.

Probably the most outstanding features of the car are the hand-formed, gracefully executed, upswept and canted tailfins. Under the fins, '56 Dodge taillights are worked into

the design. There is not even a hint of a "tacked-on" look.

The front end has been reworked, and a most unusual grille has been floated in the oval opening. The headlights are frenched, and scoops have been cut in the forward end of the front fenders. The rear fender skirts have been opened to form scoops and these are trimmed with chromed bars.

The interior is finished in rolled and pleated red and white vinyl, trimmed with gold beading.

A Little Bit Of Paint Goes A Long Way

NOSE JOB

Cars produced in the years immediately following the Second World War were bulky, big, and had a style that didn't endear themselves to the young people of the time. Yet an automobile of any description was better than none. Such was this four-door Buick, taken over by a fellow with young ideas.

Besides the customary lowering techniques applied, some well-placed scallops and a little side trim make this 1947 Buick appear somewhat longer than its actual dimensions. The lower section of the grille has been formed by hand, and the rear fenders have been reshaped.

Accessory items include twin side exhaust stacks, 1958 Cadillac wheel discs and spotlights. The exterior is jet black, trimmed with green-gold scallops.

To dress up the interior, white vinyl fastened with contrasting green buttons is used on the seats and door panels.

CRAZY COUPE

Nothing Could Be Finer Than To Own This Forty-Niner

One of the nicer grease machines of the early '50s is this 1949 Ford two-door, styled for show and for the road. The custom offers all the extra conveniences that made it popular with the young people of the period. It was one of the first custom jobs to have a TV set nestled under the right side of the dash.

It's a crowd pleaser. Its molded-in grille shell contains horizontal chromed bars in front of chrome mesh. Twin airscoops have been cut half way back on the hood.

A dramatic lowering job has been done. This involved body channeling and lowering of the frame. Ground clearance is almost zero. Side trim consists of two '55 Ford chrome pieces fitted together; one has been reversed. Mercury bumper guard bullets are used on smoothed-over bumpers.

Other features are: twin side-mounted exhaust stacks, special spinner hubcaps, twin spotlights, and unusual paint scalloping. A completely upholstered luggage compartment provides a nice finishing touch to the car.

One of the more spectacular convertibles of the '50s customizing era is this 1950 Olds machine.

A low silhouette has been accomplished by chopping the top four inches, and the other modifications put this custom in a class by itself. The grille is from a '54 Chevy. It "floats" in the molded oval. Headlights are frenched in, using Buick components. Taillights are a combination of Cadillac and '56 Chrysler parts. Scoops are cut into the hood, which has been reshaped and contoured at the front. Another decorative scoop has been added at the rear fenders, and these are highlighted by chrome horizontal bars.

The interior is done in maroon and white vinyl and custom maroon carpeting on the floor. Wine-colored lacquer completes the picture.

RACY ROCKET

Olds 98 Is Chopped, Lowered And Streamlined

Customizing often took months to complete. The owner of this machine spent three years in restyling the 1950 Ford Club Coupe to his satisfaction. Once complete, it made a big splash on the local Toledo, Ohio, circuit.

The biggest modification was the chopping of the top by a full five inches. That took months to accomplish. Other changes involve a redesigned grille oval, highlighted by the installation of three bullets, fashioned from a '53 Ford grille. The oval itself has been molded and rounded with the lower pan welded in to give the assembly that desired one-piece look. The front bumper, though stock, was rechromed after all the attaching bolts were molded in. To complete the new look of the front end, the hood has been nosed and the headlights frenched. Twin spots also were added.

Buick side trim is used effectively to separate the white and gold two-tone paint job. The interior has been completely reupholstered in gold and white vinyl.

Birds Of A Feather

Two Customizers Create Twin T-Birds

Almost—but not quite—identical twin '57 Thunderbirds were created by a couple of friends who also were car enthusiasts. Common to both T-Birds are Edsel taillights, fitted neatly into the restyled rear fenders.

Both also have roof vents: one has been borrowed from a '58 Pontiac Bonneville; the other from a '58 Chevy Impala. Both use Corvette grilles instead of the stock Ford styling, and both are equipped with '57 Dodge Lancer hubcaps.

Doors have been modified for electric push-button operation, and the side trim has been removed to provide a clean appearance.

Blue Bird

Grille From T-Bird—
Robin's-Egg Blue

The first thing you notice about this 1953 Ford Victoria is the beautiful paint—pearlescent robin's-egg blue. Then you begin to see all the other modifications that make the car look so clean.

The grille shell is from a '58 Thunderbird, modified with chrome tubing at the center. The hood has been nosed.

Original chrome fixtures have been removed (the doors now operate electrically), but the teardrop spots add some sparkle. They've been given a two-tone blue paint treatment. Additional glitter is provided by the chrome reverse wheels.

The trunk has been decked, and the custom taillight lenses have been tunneled.

Inside, the upholstery is blue and white vinyl, rolled and pleated.